Perfect Mess

Bernadette Cremin

Biscuit Publishing

Published by Biscuit Publishing Ltd., 2006

Copyright © Bernadette Cremin 2006

The right of Bernadette Cremin to be identified
as the author of this work has been asserted
by her in accordance with the Copyright,
Designs & Patents Act 1988

A catalogue for this book is
available from the British Library

First published in Great Britain by
Biscuit Publishing Ltd., 2006
PO Box 123, Washington,
Newcastle upon Tyne
NE37 2YW

ISBN 1-903914-27-2

Typeset by Mike Wilson, Bridlington

Cover design by Anthony Bratley

Printed and bound in Great Britain by
Jasprint Ltd., Tyne & Wear

For

Mum, Dad and Fish
(Happy 70th Ma!)

Acknowledgements

Acknowledgements are due to the following:

Poetry News Horizon (Blue Nose Poets) Pulsar Epilepsy Review WEA Outside Left (Halfpenny Press Eire) Pathade (Eire) The Real Mc Coy (Out of the West) Sensual Assassins (State Art) The Sensitively Thin Bill of the Shag (Biscuit) Insideskin (ACE)

I would also like to thank the late Michael Donaghy for his considered opinion and kind time. John O'Donaghue for his merciless wit and contentious criticism!! Roddy Lumsden for his keen eye and Anthony Bratley for his technical prowess patience and treasured company.

I am also grateful to ACE for their continued advice and support but most of all I thank 'God's mysterious ways'

Perfect Mess

	Page
Divas	1
Party	2
Grafitti	3
Tangerine	4
The builder	5
Ripening	6
Other side of the cloud	7
Portfolio	8
Happy ever after	9
Long story	10
Guessing	11
Thin curtain	12
Leaving John	13
Perfect mess	14
Kaiser Strasse	15
Nowness	16
Fruit for rumours	17
Heirloom	18
Widow	19
For the kids	20
Speechless	21
Brave enough	22
Black swan	23
Roadside roses	24
Quarry tiles	25
Guilty fist	26
Taste	27
The dock	28
Turquoise cocktail	29
Vodka and Valium	30
Pale roses	31
White ink	32
Do not touch	33
Licking dead bodies	34
Still	35
Redundant	36
Rush hour	37
Cliché	38
Tame chaos	39
The interview	40

Divas

Every weekend we waited:
for the milk train from Euston
broken chocolate machines
read graffiti backwards
on corrugated shop fronts
our stockings danced
into ladders and ash

and...

Every weekend he waited:
Bob the Busker with Bob the Dog;
coppers in a patchwork bowler
his saxophone bruised music
that curled my gut like sex
and melancholic lyrics sung
too beautifully out of tune.

Party

I stayed to hide inside the party
to watch the space

between things happening
stared into brutal music

asked anonymous lyrics to explain.
Tried too hard to fancy the pseudo-someone

with a fluorescent Mohican,
his girlfriend, my chances.

I left when there was nowhere to go
and fumbled home up the Kings Road

in a yesterday-dress and bare feet
chastised by October frost.

A van, two vans and an S reg'
passed at dawn speed

as each streetlight spluttered,
off.

Graffiti

I cried
in the toilet
at Piccadilly

read adverts
for underage sex,
refuge from abuse

untangled the nonsence
left by crimson lipstick
across white ceramic tiles:

clumsy mobile numbers
initials in smeared hearts
and the four letter word

that tore mine out.

Tangerine

Monday, five months of texts agreed we should
rendezvous in a lay-by. You left a
marriage at home, I wore nervous perfume
and your favourite colour, hoped it might
remind you of Austria, tequila,
the backseat of Darren's Cortina, how
in love we thought we were. It is Friday
now and I sit in Sainsbury's car park,

play with matches, rewind, count backwards from
one hundred in French and back again. Yes,
I could text, apologise, make a joke
of it, deny I listen to Lloyd Cole
deliberately but... You shouldn't have
kissed me. I shouldn't have worn tangerine.

The builder

I've started speaking French
to myself in supermarket queues

analysing Bjork's lyrics for clues
and hidden meanings since

since he walked into last Tuesday
and helped himself to my fantasy.

(Men like him are conceived
beneath grinning moons.)

He has no idea that I peel him
through the bedroom window,

trace his edge against cement
hunting him for scars.

He has no idea he makes me feel
content as a child suckling pink

when I imagine him breathing
somewhere else, wearing creases,

taking the second hand
of his watch for granted,

wondering what angles his limbs sleep in,
what his profile looks like on white sheets.

But my favourite daydream is him
wet shaving, odourless soap, a steady hand.

Carving his jawbone,
a patient blade.

Ripening

He's the one
I was warned against,
but he's the part of myself
I like best.

We were just ripening;
young love strutting
down Queen Street
dressed in a night out

laughing out loud
at tacky souvenir shops
and tourists robbed
by polystyrene fish and chips.

He was last seen in a rumour
discussing Sartre
with fresh air
on Brighton beach but...

sometimes I can convince me
that I still catch a glimpse
of him hitchhiking
on a seagulls wing

hear his smile harmonise
with ghost notes left behind
by a busking guitar string
in the Pavilion gardens

and smell his unease weave
through the haze of black coffee
and sandalwood joss sticks
in North Lane cafes.

Touch the moment again
... that changed everything
in the macabre silences
of Market Street mime artists.

He's the one
I was warned against,
but he's that part of myself
I like best.

Other side of the cloud

Fucking the stranger
would have been easier
but when my conscience stretched it just could not get that
far...

a ride in his spiteful car
inappropriately close lips
in a punch bag club

pinched by white wine
was my last minute ticket
to the other side of the cloud

to lie on anonymous linen
in a bright hotel room
and sleep a plane away.

Portfolio

He was a reason
the excuse to leave that party
a bad acid trip,
patchouli, Glenfiddich,
hands that kneaded the dark.

He was a twin, a Dutch surname
Egyptian lime cologne
a loom spun Tibetan rug
peacock blue and cerise stitches
hung from six inch nails.

He was a bed-sit in Chester Street
on the side of town that kept my mum awake
and why I lay naked under a cedar tree
while he took moody photos of me
for the portfolio under his bed.

Happy ever after

A blonde rose stared out of the calendar
accusingly. The pendulum counted
second thoughts, as time slowly surrendered
me to a handsome man and lavender
bridesmaid. But I had planned the accident-

left a butt smudged with my sisters lipstick
under the wingback chair, guilty as red.
My pulse flirted as I struck the match, touched
the hem, and nailed the smell of crackling
taffeta to the air. Indifferently.

Long story

Interflora woke her
with a blush of odourless roses
from her pinstriped son Alexander

the unshaven courier fizzed
in the frostbitten air, and though
her deafness stirred his words

she smelt a wish on his breath
and remembered handsome,
a lifetime, a long time ago:

(The pink dress that made her father cross,
the winkle pickers she peeled herself out of,
initials carved into oak by her first love.)

She spends her birthdays alone, on a bench
next to the broken pond pulling crusts
into kind sizes for storms of pigeons

as February pinches like new shoes
and ice brews in the corners of everywhere
hunting for accidents.

Guessing

She used to …
with the only man
she'll want to marry

she still recalls
his thick cuticles
the jet fleck

in his right eye,
the mess they left
under the bed.

Now she pretends to…
alone. Dials 141
before ringing

his answerphone
to say nothing
and if Jayne picks it up

she waits just that moment
longer than enough
to keep her guessing.

Thin curtain

I went to bed early last night
with the Sellotaped spine paperback
I underline in green,
(scribble in the margins
as if coaxing something out.)

Our unmade bedroom smelt of excuses
and kicked-off shoes, so I lit an incense stick
and traced the shape of smoke falling in
between the cracks of our mix-n-match furniture
cluttered with the 'us' between you and me:

mug rings, bits and bobs of something's
the uncertain clock broken by an argument,
the contents of your emptied pocket;
sixteen pence in loose change, wallet, keys,
and today's till receipt from Sainsbury's
for the usual: egg roll, cherry coke, King Size Twix.

I went to bed early last night
leaving you to grope the evening
for stimulating company on your own:
late night B-rate pornography
and blended whisky again.

You trip-tip-toed in late.
I feigned sleep to avoid another faked headache
and watched you undress in the dim street light
that sneaks in through our thin curtain
that can't hide either side anymore.

Leaving John

I hired Stan Jones (& son)
their blue van, a Tuesday afternoon
to move nine years in April
to a one bedroom flat
a number 5 bus ride away.

Stan wore a black fingernail,
a beer – gut – stretched – T - shirt
stained by the poll tax riots he still fights
with sixth-form politics, holding on
to a someone he never was.

Now I don't recognise the life
I've packed and labelled too neat:
Keep Upright, Breakable, Handle with Care.
(Stan has no idea I'm leaving a husband
(polite conversation doesn't ask).

Moving was Marion L Spencer's choice,
I imagine her naked too often:
stockings, Chanel flesh, green eyes
kissing John's midlife crisis goodnight
in expense paid rooms.

I pretend to be interested in Stan's new girlfriend:
redhead, loves curry, three kids,
then he grunts for the choc-chip biscuits
he finished a milky three heaped spoons ago
and that memory back flips back in:

her earring in the washing machine. Typical. Gold.

Perfect mess

They met at a party
where surnames
were not invited

neither had
expected this,
tender accident.

Now they meet in alibis
to pool their egos
and unfold loves dark art

like a ballerinas spine,
in a rented room
with green muslin curtains

where their secret lies
under the bed.
They are the perfect mess:

powerless as ice in vodka
polluted yet beautiful,
petrol on water.

Kaiser Strasse
(for Michael Donaghy)

Heat has kidnapped the attic. Vindictive.
Janis Joplin is bouncing off the walls,
his eyes close as he waits for the needle
to back-flip that chorus in scratched vinyl:
make me feel like a natural woman
make me feel like a natural woman
lyrics that drag him back to Jade's bed-sit:
her vodka temper, widowed lingerie,
Klimt prints, bitten kisses, wounded music.
Standing on the balcony he throws three . . .
wishes at tarmac, hopes she's been blinded,
that her sleep aches and he still stains her sheets.
He needs mangled hotel rooms now, raw prayer.
The stubborn view of Berlin, simmering.

Nowness

Why did I invite myself
to a town I can't spell

a cheap hotel with old soap
and psychedelic curtains

try to convince myself
it would mend me,

pretend I'll write poetry
diet, lose a few pounds

and return to Brighton
with a suspicious glow.

But I'm just as lost
on this prettier beach

where the horizon flatlines
and the tide can't sleep.

I watch a blind child
eat an ice-cream

and arrest,
nowness.

Threaten the weather,
take deep breaths of the view

and argue with postcards,
try to unravel a scribble

of gulls above
as they swoon in and out

of each others shadows,
failing to fool love.

Fruit for rumours

I sit on the cracked plastic swing
in a playground I found

a few months ago
in a bus window:

half swinging, half not
and watch evening

sign its senile will
in lard coloured clouds

that gang up like cancer
overhead.

The threat of rain is exhausting
I want, to still smoke.

I didn't notice tea time
empty the climbing frame,

lose its mitten in the grass,
leave the hopscotch-scuffed tarmac

behind till tomorrow after school.
I sit, half swing, half not

and listen to sounds knit
like skin healing.

A woman alone
in a dim playground

I have become,
fruit for rumours.

Heirloom
(for John O' Donaghue)

While I swelled my Mother's belly
a tumour helped itself to her,
I was born premature
an hour before she died.

I've come to know her through avoided questions,
overheard conversations, Uncle Eamon's moods,
as the woman who wore black and white stripes
and ate grey ice cream in her honeymoon photos.

She's the blackthorn rosary that dad gave me
on my twenty first birthday in a simple box,
the christening shawl she had crocheted
and folded in tissue like a prayer;

It smelt of imagined lavender,
a gentle mess of untamed wool
that Dad wrapped my violet child in
when the white coffin arrived.

Widow

Things must be simple now,
I am incapable
of edges

please forgive
the daisies
in his ashtray

the stubborn fug
of pipe smoke
that hangs...

pitiful as Jesus.
Please do not touch
that impossible colour

kidnapped by the glaze
of that ugly vase
because...

he said he heard a violin
when he stared long enough
into the livid brushstroke

that licked it's long neck
and I loved him
for such petite reasons...

...Yes I know somewhere
a child is being bent,
a car crash is drawing...

its last breath but
things must be simple now,
I am incapable of edges.

For the kids

We sat on the wrong side of sympathy

as Dr Scott's manicured words
outlined the shadow that has crawled
around your lung like spiteful ivy
since last autumn.

For the last time we faced
that painting in her consulting room:
'Mountain' (oil on canvas). Abstract.
Signed in a contrived hand, underlined.

For a moment truth made the view bigger.
Outside, London was still happening,
red, amber, green.
Brixton was planning its tea.

You fussed with your cuff like a truant
as the diagnosis was disguised
in plain English for us to take home
to the kids, a gift-wrapped grenade.

Forever gracious you offered to drive
knowing I am petrified of twilight.
We sat, gridlocked, then as if it didn't matter
you leant forward, let a violin out of the radio.

We pulled into the drive, parked.
Chloe's bike was still against the shed
where yesterday had left it.
Now is where the end begins:

I'll start to collect your silhouettes,
fingerprints left on glass and plastic,
your discarded shadows, left-over profiles
and rough sketches I'll never show you

for the portrait I'll paint,
David (oil on canvas). Abstract.
To hang at that sly angle
only you would understand.

Speechless

Her boiled voice gargles
wrong answers to his crossword clues
he feeds her mashed banana
with a plastic spoon,

picks out soft centres,
peels fruit with a patient blade,
tidies her bedside cabinet
every evening before he leaves.

He invents gossip and well wishes
from neighbours who never visit
and repeats the same over animated tale
about a cat she can't remember since

her head collapsed.

                        But when they sit against
                        November bruised windows,
                        words have no words
                        for their crooked silhouette;

                        wrapped in the scarf of starlings
                        that carves its path toward West Pier
                        her hand in his, a broken wing
                        that hangs between them.

A dazed angel.

Brave enough

You are vulnerable
as the lack of light
folded in a white
handkerchief.

I tread the undertow
with you, and though
you hold me under
I hear you screaming.

You are brave enough
to be human . . .
and it touches me
in a place that hurts

more than beauty.

Black Swan

She taught him
how to let her kiss
the cusp of his neck

he taught her
how to wait, how to sit
still until it hurt

but neither of them
trusted the black swan,
the beautiful contradiction

so they sucked thorns
and hunted for other words
that sounded like love…

but nostalgia
is a strange flavour
echoes and broken cobwebs

a ghost in the mouth
that hungers for faith
in the wisdom of dust

unable to forget the aftertaste
of a day that walked barefoot
in the last breath of autumn

an evening that faced west
as a mauve sunset genuflected
to an unborn morning

and the night that candlelight
dared them to stretch beyond
themselves and touch,

the lack of nothingness between them.

Roadside roses

He buys her time
with roadside roses
and guilt trips

looking for himself
in the broken promises
he leaves for her to pluck.

He doesn't notice:
she hasn't worn weekday lipstick
since the stitches dissolved…

dissolved like the sugar lumps
she watches drown in coffee shop
spoons where sits for hours,

safe among the trivial strangers
she trusts more than herself.
There she presses tenderness,

teases the fresh bruises
that turned indigo overnight
while she lays awake,

raw as a butcher's window,
blooding cotton like a virgin,
keeping their little secret under the bed.

Quarry tiles

He's spilt her on the kitchen floor
she lies curled toward the sun
watching the warm leak
from her temple crawl
toward the door like a fat worm.

He goes upstairs to change his shirt
leaving her to count the ninety-eight
stripes in the curtain again
the hem still needs mending
she'll get some red cotton, tomorrow.

She hears the cough,
phlegm-spit-in-the-toilet, flush -
knows he'll be back in twenty-seven steps
to smoke a Marlboro to the filter
sink another Tennants Extra then . . .

fuck off anywhere.
When he leaves she'll drink tea
with dirty breakfast things,
get dressed, mop up the mess
before the kids get in from school.

Guilty fist

The just qualified doctor

blamed the baby
said it was 'respiratory difficulty'
mummy said nothing.

Down the nursery corridor
they blessed her empty daughter
in a tepid incubator.

Mummy unplugged her,
doctor told her to,
nothing he could do and…

the machine stopped breathing
that moment will beat
mummy's conscience like a dog.

Outside, under the casualty fire exit
daddy sucked cigarettes to death,
strangled pink carnations in a guilty fist

that always forgives itself…
mummy said nothing
watching her daughter, turn blue.

Taste

From a teased distance
he pays immaculate attention
to the blonde shadows
he peels for perfume.

His grin is keen as hurt,
a buckled skull bone-shaven,
a dead straight navy hairline
one malicious scar.

He rents himself
when he feels contemptuous,
milks stale strangers,
remembers the taste.

The dock

Fossilised terraces,
muscular pavements,
leather men lace
the docks sweating neck,
woo the swollen ocean
into it with hungry songs.

From the quay
an uncombed boy throws
stones into the wash
of a cargo going home;
skims a wish...
across the nomadic tides.

From a spluttering tug
a beer belly with clatty whiskers
jeers at a bottle blonde
in red chiselled heels
as she stalks St Patrick's bridge,
hunting callous hands.

Torquoise cocktail

The email read:

oral and anal
Trent hotel
8pm punctual
six hundred non- negotiable
key available from seven
room 591 in the name of Blondyn

Specifics:

red leather gimp kit, total silence
in Times New Roman 10:
The John font.
The Broadsheet font.
The Small Print font.
The Appointment from the Hospital font.

I'd never worked the Trent before:
The Sherbet fountain,
The Powder Tower
where cufflinks wink, ice grins,
and staff say very little
in all the right places.

I arrived perfectly early
sat legs crossed in the lustrous bar
and sipped a turquoise cocktail
to conjure the mood,
left an ignorant tip,
collected the key.

Vodka and Valium

Liam didn't stir,
snug among the curls in his cot
unaware the day had cracked

downstairs I heard
Anne and Auntie Kathleen
fumbling with sympathy

it felt just like the morning
Uncle Eamon got out of prison,
moved in, kipped on the sofa

smoked skinny roll-ups
and swigged stout
in the green chair all day.

I got up, cold lino,
my breath swelled uncertain
in the too early air.

I took each stair suspiciously
as if hunting Santa and saw Anne
through the banister rails trying to cry.

She shouted to go and get a cigarette
to steady her nerves so I did;
Piccadilly untipped, the bitter pinch

of baccy on my tongue,
that first blunt lug,
I put the kettle on.

Dad came down, barefeet and string vest
dragging unfinished sleep
and a fog of Old Holburn

Anne said Uncle Damien was found
in a Jury's hotel room:
vodka and Valium.

Anne said it was a blessing,
Dad said nothing, just coughed,
phoned work, rolled another smoke.

Pale roses

This photograph
has kept the years
under glass, sunlight's
smuggled the colours
from her dress,
the innocence
she wore under it
and held that moment
hostage

faded the host
of pale roses
that caged
his garden,
the brittle petals
and twisted stems
that strained
to touch
anywhere else

when he pruned
her smile and drove
her small fingers
around him in the dark
forcing her eyes
to take root in the lens.
Now, she hunts for loss
in the negative
of her own reflection.

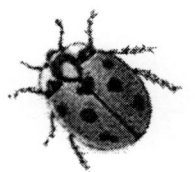

White ink

He was the reason for cravats

cuff links and pinkie rings,
wore green Italian leather shoes
and was everything vodka promised
to the right mood.

He was exactly handsome
and blurred our evening rehearsals
with a Portuguese wine
I mispronounced on purpose.

He swelled my dressing room
with Cuban cigar smoke,
a suggestion of cologne
and jokes about his double knotted wife.

He taught me the purpose of curtains,
how to bone a soliloquy till it fit on a cuff,
scratch a quote into my watchstrap with a compass,
and how to write a killerline in white ink

across my wrist.

Do not touch

He traced the moon with his eyes closed for her
licked her fresh skin with pond-coloured satin

knew how to seduce youth with black perfume
but coaxed her too close and bruised his conscience.

At first he could bribe the truth that curdled
his gut, hush the fear of getting caught but

when sleep began to hide behind the sky
and drag each night toward dawn by the hair

bending every moment he spent alone
he knew that her smell would never be gone-

it was beyond him to forget how his
manipulative wit had folded her,

how the palm of her hand held his future,
how she could put out his pulse with three words.

Licking dead bodies

The prospect of sleep is ridiculous
as the nursery rhymes adolescence
left under the bed...

did I really leave my eyelids
in your hand when the train pulled
you out of sight?

Now, when I close my eyes
I see blind sheep head butting fences,
biting lumps out of the furniture,

their rubbery tongues blooding dreams
like raw liver under a leather bound foot.
Now, night bursts the dark, digs its own grave

in a whiskey-pillow that still slurs
your apology; a dead body for me to lick.
Did I really leave my eyelids in your hand?

Still

Life woke up late again,
laid perfectly still and stared
into each inch of ceiling

listened to manic traffic
that stilled summer
like smart wasps

watched the afternoon tiptoe
across the room indifferently.
Everything was still Tuesday.

Rachel's advice
still didn't make sense:
exercise green veg', fresh air.

Rachel hasn't called since…
but still sends a lemon rose
hand-wrapped in white tissue

on special occasions
from the florists in Bastille Street
that smells of adultery.

The letter from Japan still hasn't come
but every day junk mail
waits like conscience,

creeping in with the manila bills
at that still-time just before
a day begins, to smell.

Redundant

I eat tuna from a tin,
watch London Road
fuelling tempers,
wonder what the green car
had for breakfast.
Why I care.

Through a must-wash window
the 5a throws up into the bus stop
then moans on and on
to the same feng shui beige office blocks
and chrome shops as every day
at approximately 8.06.

The kettle clicks:
another day begins,
without me.

Rush hour

Headlights gridlocked
in wet windscreens,
coats jamming paving stones
shunting home
to migraines,
junk-mail,
unmade beds.

A No-One begging
briefcases
for loose change.
The same navy pinstripe
slicing its way
to another double malt
on the rocks.

Cliché

Love is why white
roses bother to open,
why eyes conjure
and sunsets swell
the horizon,
Van Gogh orange.

It smudges lipstick,
ladders stockings,
leaves grass stains
and mascara running,
stands alone on the
platform waving till

the train dissolves in a bend.
It's the final step off
the edge of yourself,
where lunatic and lilac
dovetail into a moment
that is…

frail as patience,
a buttered tightrope
a glass hinge,
where limbs knit
in the dim left
by a shy moon.

It knows when to leave
what is meant unsaid,
when to leave it, white
can temper anger
and nurse trust
without words.

Love is what skin feels just before, touch.

Tame chaos

Somewhere deep outside me
a bird's song is broken
by its own breath

leaving only silence
to tame the chaos
into one image:

a finger on a guitar string
old black skin hanging
from a buckled knucklebone

so I hold it, hold it
hold it deep inside until it fits,
fits like a kiss.

The interview

The receptionist is anorexic

has a hint of hip
rhubarb cheeks:
a blonde ghost that digs
itself out of its own throat.

The office is serious

an oxblood chesterfield
mahogany bookcase
leather-bound classics
a gabardine man with olive eyes.

I wear snakeskin slingbacks

to exaggerate my negligible ankles
translucent seamed stockings,
ivory silk fitted blouse
pearl button at the neck

and sit

teasing the nipple
of my suspender belt
through rouge cashmere
I never do

wear knickers to interviews.